EAT LI
BOOK SE]

Eat Like a Local- Sarasota: Sarasota Florida Food Guide

I have lived in the Sarasota area since 1998 and learned about many great places that I want to try. –Conoal

EAT LIKE A LOCAL-CONNECTICUT: Connecticut Food Guide

This a great guide to try different places in Connecticut to eat. Can't wait to try them all! The author is awesome to explore and try all these different foods/drinks. There are places I didn't know they existed until I got this book and I am a CT resident myself! –Caroline J. H.

EAT LIKE A LOCAL- LAS VEGAS: Las Vegas Nevada Food Guide

Perfect food guide for any tourist traveling to Vegas or any local looking to go outside their comfort zone! –TheBondes

Eat Like a Local-Jacksonville: Jacksonville Florida Food Guide

Loved the recommendations. Great book from someone who knows their way around Jacksonville. –Anonymous

EAT LIKE A LOCAL- COSTA BRAVA: Costa Brava Spain Food Guide

The book was very well written. Visited a few of the restaurants in the book, they were great! Sylvia V.

Eat Like a Local-Sacramento: Sacramento California Food Guide

As a native of Sacramento, Emerald's book touches on some of our areas premier spots for food and fun. She skims the surface of what Sacramento has to offer recommending locations in historical, popular areas where even more jewels can be found. –Katherine G.

Eat Like a Local

EAT LIKE
A LOCAL-
VANCOUVER

Vancouver Canada Food Guide

Amanda Lawrence

BOOK DESCRIPTION

Are you excited about planning your next trip? Do you want an edible experience? Would you like some culinary guidance from a local? If you answered yes to any of these questions, then this Eat Like a Local book is for you. Eat Like a Local - Vancouver by author Amanda Lawrence offers the inside scoop on food on the best restaurants in Vancouver Canada. Culinary tourism is an important aspect of any travel experience. Food has the ability to tell you a story of a destination, its landscapes, and culture on a single plate. Most food guides tell you how to eat like a tourist. Although there is nothing wrong with that, as part of the Eat Like a Local series, this book will give you a food guide from someone who has lived at your next culinary destination.

In these pages, you will discover advice on having a unique edible experience. This book will not tell you exact addresses or hours but instead will give you excitement and knowledge of food and drinks from a local that you may not find in other travel food guides.

Eat like a local. Slow down, stay in one place, and get to know the food, people, and culture. By the time you finish this book, you will be eager and prepared to travel to your next culinary destination.

OUR STORY

Traveling has always been a passion of the creator of the Eat Like a Local book series. During Lisa's travels in Malta, instead of tasting what the city offered, she ate at a large fast-food chain. However, she realized that her traveling experience would have been more fulfilling if she had experienced the best of local cuisines. Most would agree that food is one of the most important aspects of a culture. Through her travels, Lisa learned how much locals had to share with tourists, especially about food. Lisa created the Eat Like a Local book series to help connect people with locals which she discovered is a topic that locals are very passionate about sharing. So please join me and: Eat, drink, and explore like a local.

TABLE OF CONTENTS

DEDICATION

This book is dedicated to Rachel Delamorandiere-Upchan (1992-2021), a loving mother, home cook and foodie for the ages. Thank you for introducing me to cooking and a love for food. Even though you're gone I know you'll always be with me, making sure I order the dessert.

ABOUT THE AUTHOR

Amanda is a nanny, foodie and experienced world traveller who likes to experience other countries through food. She passionately believes that every culture tells a unique story through the ingredients, spices and methods of preparing food. There is so much to learn in a dish, more than meets the eye. Amanda likes to travel as sustainably as possible, making sure to support the local economy along her travels.

Amanda has travelled to over 15 countries and she currently lives in Vancouver, Canada. When she is not working or trying new recipes at home you can find her hiking the mountains of BC, trying to catch a wave or uncovering more hidden gems in Vancouver.

HOW TO USE THIS BOOK

The goal of this book is to help culinary travelers either dream or experience different edible experiences by providing opinions from a local. The author has made suggestions based on their own knowledge. Please do your own research before traveling to the area in case the suggested locations are unavailable.

Travel Advisories: As a first step in planning any trip abroad, check the Travel Advisories for your intended destination.
https://travel.state.gov/content/travel/en/traveladvisories/traveladvisories.html

FROM THE PUBLISHER

Traveling can be one of the most important parts of a person's life. The anticipation and memories that you have are some of the best. As a publisher of the *Eat Like a Local*, Greater Than a Tourist, as well as the popular *50 Things to Know* book series, we strive to help you learn about new places, spark your imagination, and inspire you. Wherever you are and whatever you do I wish you safe, fun, and inspiring travel.

Lisa Rusczyk Ed. D.
CZYK Publishing

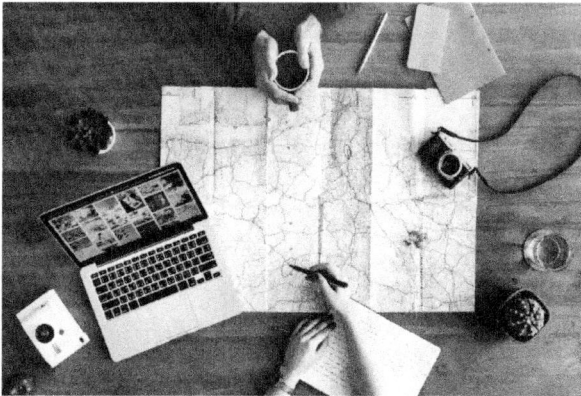

"I love just how beautiful Vancouver is. I mean everywhere you look it's just mountains and ocean."

- Emma Bell

Vancouver is a relatively young city (like almost all of Canada) compared to the rest of the world but that doesn't mean it is lacking. It is a multifaceted city that continues to meet and exceed the expectations of its residents and visitors.

Moving to Vancouver was one of the most exciting and spontaneous things that I have done. I always loved the mountains and hiking and I knew Vancouver would be the perfect city for me. Not only did it's natural beauty convince me to go hiking almost every weekend, it's abundance of year round activities keeps me out of the house almost every evening. I mean who can say they have been skiing and surfing in one day. Didn't know that was possible? Yeah, Vancouver has that down pat.

I'll have to be honest though, I was a bit underwhelmed with the food scene when I initially arrived. It seemed as I wandered the downtown core I only saw chain restaurants and cafes and it was underwhelming. Only after living here for a while did I start to be able to look past that and see what was hidden in plain sight! It was like putting on a pair of 3D glasses and finally being able to see the whole picture. I was pleasantly shocked to finally be able to uncover Vancouver's food scene that is well hidden, unless you know where to look. The multicultural restaurants, bars and cafes are abundant across the city and new ones seem to open every day. It seems like the possibility to explore is endless, for adventurers who are looking to discover.

I hope that you find these tips useful in your travels here and you can put on your 3D glasses and see the whole picture right away (without having to wait months like I did).

Vancouver
British Columbia, Canada

Vancouver
Canada
Climate

	High	Low
January	44	37
February	47	38
March	51	40
April	56	44
May	63	49
June	67	54
July	72	58
August	72	58
September	66	53
October	57	47
November	49	41
December	44	37

GreaterThanaTourist.com

Temperatures are in Fahrenheit degrees.
Source: NOAA

1. WHY VISIT VANCOUVER

Vancouver is Canada's 3rd largest city and it's metropolitan area covers 115 sq km. Due to its prime location at the bottom of the north shore mountains, right beside the ocean and it's relatively temperate climate it makes it the perfect Canadian city to visit all year round! Average temperatures hover from 34°F in the winter to 77°F in the summer. Of course global warming is affecting these temperatures slightly so it might be as cold as 26°F in winter or 86°F in the summer. Vancouver is a popular choice for those who would like to come to Canada in the winter months as the climate is agreeable all year round, as opposed to other areas of Canada like Calgary or Ottawa that can reach -22°F in the winter months.

When most people think about Vancouver they think of its proximity to beautiful mountain ranges, ocean beaches and its Pacific temperate rainforests. Some popular activities in Vancouver are hiking, beach volleyball, stand up paddle boarding, skiing, snowboarding, cycling and the list goes on! If you love to get up and go while on vacation it is the place to be. When you look from the outside in, Vancouver's food scene may not look like much, in the popular touristy areas you can find many chain restaurants and cafes that you would see in any other Canadian or US city, but people often underestimate Vancouver's food scene.

Vancouver is an underrated foodie's dream. Not only does it boast the best seafood west of Quebec but it offers restaurants and unique dishes from all over the world (and it isn't very loud about it). Vancouver keeps its foodie underbelly well hidden, but it's there if you care to look.

2. THE RIGHT TIMING

In order to fully explore all that Vancouver has to offer you need at least one week in the city and surrounding area. If you plan to take day trips from Vancouver to popular spots like Tofino, Victoria, Okanagan Valley, Squamish or Whistler I would recommend two weeks. There are plenty of restaurants, bars, hikes, museums, markets, parks and history in Vancouver to keep you busy for weeks! The best time to visit Vancouver would be during the summer months, July and August but those are peak tourist months and the city can become a bit crowded. You can still catch some nice weather in May and June as well as September and early October but make sure you're prepared for some rain.

3. CURRENCY TO CARRY

In Canada we use the Canadian Dollar. You will find the bank notes quite easy to differentiate from one another due to their bright colours. There are no 1$ notes and anything less than 2$ comes as coins. In Canada the price shown does not include tax so expect to pay 15% more at the register, for example if it costs 1$ on the shelf it will be about 1.15$ at the check out. Credit and debit cards are more than welcome as well as apple pay at almost all restaurants, cafes and even chip stands and food trucks. ATMs can be found scattered around popular areas or you can walk into any bank and use the bank atm (for a fee). Fun fact! In 2011 Canada introduced plastic money! So no need to worry about forgetting your bills in your pocket at the beach!

4. TIPS ABOUT TIPS

It is customary anywhere in Canada to leave a tip for your server at a restaurant. Servers make less than minimum wage in Canada and more often than not rely on tips to supplement their wage. Most people leave a 15% tip for ok service, and 18-20% for great service. Of course if you are having an awful experience with your server and you are very unhappy with your experience it would be alright to not leave a tip. In cafes, food trucks or food stands it is also customary to leave a little tip (less than a restaurant) 10% would be average. Debit and credit machines may prompt you to choose a certain percent of tip but you can also choose a dollar option and pick a custom amount.

5. IMPORTANT ITEMS TO PACK

Vancouver's weather can change fairly quickly but it's safe to say it may rain at least once (if not most of the time) when you visit. Pack a good waterproof jacket, waterproof shoes and an umbrella for sure. If you come during the summer shorts, tank tops and Tshirt's are a good choice and for winter longer pants, and sweaters are sure to keep you warm and dry. Make sure to include a good pair of walking or running shoes, as the city is quite large and walking from one place to another might be the most efficient way to get where you're going. People in Vancouver dress however they would like to, but please be mindful as there are dress codes for places of worship and fine dining restaurants.

6. WHERE TO GO?

So you've booked the tickets and packed your bag, but what neighbourhoods are worth seeing? Vancouver is a city with many hats meaning there are many places in the city if you want to be in nature, by the beach, grab a bite or go shopping and sometimes they overlap and sometimes they don't. The best neighbourhoods to grab a bite or have a drink can be scattered over the city.

7. FOOD SUGGESTIONS

Places like Davie Village or Granville can be a bit of a trek to other areas like Main Street or Kitsilano so it's important to have a bit of a plan in mind when you're going out. In addition to the neighbourhoods I mentioned above, Chinatown, Granville Island, Coal Harbour, Gastown, Yaletown and Punjabi Market are all great neighbourhoods that are worthy of a visit. Even though most neighbourhoods have plenty of variety and a good mix of bars, restaurants and cafes some neighbourhoods do it better than others. Davie Village, Granville and Chinatown are all great places to explore if you want to go out to a bar and have a grand night on the town. Kitsilano, Main Street, Punjabi Market and Granville Island are all great places to go for breakfast or lunch during the day and are less lively at night. Yaletown and Gastown are both beautiful historic neighbourhoods that are great both day and night but can be a bit more expensive than other neighbourhoods. Coal Harbour is another area that's a bit more expensive but you're also right on the Vancouver Harbour.

8. PLACES TO EAT SOLO

Dining solo can be extremely difficult for some, as we have become very accustomed to sharing meals with family and friends and aren't so accustomed to eating alone. Not everyone is up for a solo meal but sometimes there are occasions that call for it. If you would like to try a new restaurant or are traveling solo in a new city, dining alone seems inevitable. Going to restaurants that have up beat vibes and a communal feel can help ease the difficulty of dining alone and even turn it into a unique and fun experience where you can meet other people!

Hunnybee bruncheonette is a bright, earthy and open cafe/ brunch hotspot in Vancouver's downtown eastside. They offer a limited menu with a mix of light and heavier options. The space is perfect for solo diners as the bar and open patio space encourages chatter and conversation. Alternatively the bar space is a great idea if you truly want to dine alone and just enjoy your meal.

Homer St Cafe is an intimate upscale cafe in Yaletown offering a wide range of meat based dishes like fresh shucked oysters and lamb shank. The intimate size of the cafe and unique combination of

19

group tables, bar and patio seating makes it the perfect place to mingle or grab a solo fine dining experience.

Pidgin restaurant is a great place to come and sample some delightful Asian/French fusion food. With a mainly meat heavy menu designed by head chef Wesley Young and a new vegan menu brought in by chef Kym Nguyen there will be something on the table for everyone!. The Elk striploin or the Butter Poached Halibut are the way to go! The long bar area makes it a great choice if you are dining solo. Feel free to chat up the bartender over a flight of Sake or bond with your neighbour over the sous vide octopus, either way a night out at Pidgin is a night to remember!

9. PLACES TO EAT FOR TWO

Everyone seems to be racking their brains for the perfect place to take their partner, or date these days and the top 10 lists just aren't cutting it. No one wants to spend hours scrolling through their phone deciding where to eat. Whether it's a first date or a romantic evening with your loved one, you want it to be a special and memorable occasion. That's where I come in. Here is a comprehensive list of restaurants that are sure to make a great impression and even better memories.

The Shameful Tiki Room is the first place that comes to mind. This low lit cozy bar/restaurant is a great place to bring your date. Why? You may ask, the menu is loaded with small bites and plates that are begging to be shared, not to mention some of the best cocktails in the city! The fresh fruit flavours in almost every drink will have you thinking you're on a tropical island. If you're brave, order a bowl which is a drink that needs to be shared with someone (or multiple people) but beware it might get a little loud. It is bound to be a night to remember at the Shameful Tiki.

Care to take your date somewhere more elegant with an intellectual touch? Open Outcry is a cocktail bar in downtown Vancouver that looks like a page out of a Sherlock Holmes novel. The deep coloured walls, wood decor and low lighting make it the perfect place for a charcuterie board and a signature cocktail. The intimate seating makes it the prime location to bring a date.

10. PLACES TO EAT FOR A GROUP

Dining as a group can be great fun if you find the right restaurants, which can be tricky if some restaurants have limited tables or require reservations and may not have many options if people in your party have dietary restrictions. The Flying Pig in Gastown is perfect for groups, they have a beautiful communal table for groups and a delicious seasonal menu for a different experience every time you come.

Nuba serves delicious middle eastern food that can accommodate any guests dietary restrictions. They have many delicious gluten free, vegan or vegetarian meals, and something for the meat eaters too.

The Botanist is the last place I can think of when it comes to group dining but it certainly is not the least. The decor in this restaurant is a literal breath of fresh air. The floral patterns, bright open spaces and natural elements will have you feeling like you're dining in a botanical garden. The head chef showcases the delicious food that is local to the Pacific northwest, so you're in for a treat! They have great spaces for groups as well as a private room you can book for bigger events.

11. POUTINE FOR THE PEOPLE!

In major cities like Vancouver you can find this wide range of Canadian dishes and delicacies all in one place! The most popular and well known Canadian dish would have to be poutine. This hearty staple originates in Quebec and is made up of fresh fries, piping hot beef gravy and squeaky fresh cheese curds. It has quickly spread in popularity across the country and due to that popularity, poutine can be found at just about any restaurant in Vancouver (and even the ones that don't have it can probably make it for you). In Vancouver you will find two different types of poutine people: traditionalists who are trying to perfect the classic poutine and the visionaries who try to reinvent the poutine. Your choice will vary depending on what you are hungry for! If it's your first time trying poutine I would recommend going the traditional way.

For the traditional route I highly recommend La Belle Patate for some hearty stick to your bones cheese. They also offer a 20$ all you can eat poutine option, because one order is never enough! If you are looking to go on a poutine adventure you need to try Mean Poutine! This family owned business offers many different unique kinds of poutine like Southern BBQ, Vegetarian and Mean Mexicans poutines. If those options aren't jumping out at you, you can also create your own!

12. CANADIAN MAINS

Canadian cuisine is new in terms of the cuisines of the world and is rich, flavourful and usually heavy in carbohydrates and animal products. There are many unique dishes all across the country that vary depending on region, availability of ingredients and the season. Other than poutine there are many dishes that Canadians enjoy, and you can enjoy them too!

Montreal style bagels are the king of all bagels and I cannot be convinced otherwise. Polar opposite to the bready hard bottom cousins found in NYC the Montreal bagel is thinner, sweeter and more dense. They are traditionally cooked in a wood fire oven that gives it a crunchier crust and layers on the flavour. You need to stop in and grab a bagel from Rosemary Rocksalt in Kitsilano! You can try a classic Montreal bagel with a smear of cream cheese or one of their bagel sandwiches, creatively named after neighbourhoods in Vancouver! Although matter what you pick you're bound to love it.

Another favourite hailing from Montreal is the Montreal smoked meat sandwich! Made from cured beef brisket with spices this is a popular deli sandwich in Montreal that's made its way all across Canada. You can find a traditional smoked meat sandwich at Omnitsky Kosher on Oak st, served up the classic way, over a deli counter

Tourtiere is a French Canadian meat pie made with a savoury blend of meats, usually pork and veal, that originated in Quebec. For years this was a traditional pie eaten around the christmas season but has since become a staple at many pie shops across Canada.

Try the best tourtiere at Aphrodite's Organic Cafe and Pie Shop in Kitsilano. They specialize in delicious pies that are served in the cafe or can be taken home whole! They also offer Gluten free pies.

13. CANADIAN DESSERTS

Canadian desserts are a popular choice in Canada but are likely to be lesser known around the world. They usually consist of hearty, fatty ingredients like butter, sugar, whole fat milks and chocolate. Their high caloric count shouldn't count them out though! They are worth trying at least once.

Butter tarts are a Canadian dessert staple! This flakey sweet tart can be found in any Canadian household! The best butter tarts in Vancouver can be found at Tartine bread and pies. If you're looking for a butter tart with a twist try The Pie Hole in Kitsilano, they always have something interesting in the oven!

Beaver tails are the one of the most confusing deserts to say the least. I promise it isn't made out of a real beaver's tail, but rather a flat fried dough topped with a variety of toppings. You can have one that's as basic as cinnamon and sugar or crazier ones such as strawberry cheesecake or apple pie! Beavertails is a company that opened up in 1978 in Ottawa, Ontario and has since spread all over Canada. You can find their food trucks spread throughout Vancouver!

Nanaimo bars are a delicious no bake, three layer treat hailing from Nanaimo, BC. This super sweet treat made its debut in a 1953 Edith Adams prize cookbook and has stolen the hearts of all Canadians. It can be quite common to find Nanaimo bars sold in cafes all over Vancouver but they just don't taste as good unless you pick them up from a real bakery. Laurels Fine Foods in the Granville Island Market has you covered! (We will go in depth about the Granville Island Market later on). Laurels opened in 1990 and is a family owned business that designed their kitchen to be open so customers could see how the pastries were made. Pop by for a nanaimo bar and see how the pro's do it!

Last but not least is our famous maple syrup! This versatile condiment is the perfect pairing for waffles, crepes, pancakes or snow (yes snow). I would recommend trying the classic pancakes with maple syrup from The Templeton, an old school diner on Granville st. Old school diners are the best place to find some of the classics that haven't changed throughout the times. The Templeton serves up crazy versions of pancakes but you can still get the classics here.

14. SEE THE SEA

Vancouver is world famous for its seafood. With boats pulling in the daily catch almost every hour of every day it's impossible not to get the freshest seafood possible. Most seafood you try in the interior of Canada has to be flash frozen on the boat and shipped to its location by truck or train which inevitably changes the taste slightly. You can taste the difference in freshness between the two when the fresh fish comes straight from the ocean to your plate. Save for the East coast, it is some of the best you'll have in Canada.

If you are a sushi and sashimi lover you need to try the freshest fish at Sushi Bar Shu. Created by Chef Hyunki Shin with the customers' satisfaction as a top priority, Sushi Bar Shu was born. With a prix fixe menu you can find some of the highest quality fish and seafood in the Japanese style. It is truly a one of a kind experience to eat here.

Fanny Bay Oyster Bar was started by three fishermen and has since grown into a large-scale operation that now has its own oyster bars and catering service as well as selling oysters wholesale. They are committed to a tide to table experience that brings you the highest quality oysters. In addition to giving back to the communities they are also active in the protection of the marine environment. Not only does it taste good but you can feel good about eating a Fanny Bay oyster.

Go Fish is your classic takeout fish and chip restaurant on Granville Island. It's the perfect place to grab a take away cod and chips or an oyster po boy, and eat it with a beautiful view of downtown Vancouver along False Creek. Go Fish is a no frills place to come and sample some fresh Vancouver seafood!

15. INDIGENOUS DELIGHTS

Canada has a rich Indigenous history that often goes under the radar on a global scale. In recent years Indigneous and non indigenous people in Canada have been bringing forth Indigenous history, stories, art and food to the forefront. Indingenous cuisine has been a huge part of that. Indigenous cuisine is a mix of the two parts of Indigenous history in Canada: Before colonization which would consist of local game such as bison, salmon, and elk and foraged vegetables and grains like wild rice, berries, and vegetables. After colonization some new food items were introduced to Indigenous people one of them being flour, which Indigenous peoples used to make Bannock, a survival staple which has now been integrated into their cuisine.

To experience Indigenous food is to find your way back to the basics: meat, vegetables and simple spices tastefully pulled together to create something unique and rich. Salmon n' Bannock is a restaurant that blends the basics together in a new and creative way that is unique to the many first nations communities in British Columbia. On their menu you can find savoury and sweet bannock, wild game like bison and other game that rotates with the seasons as well as salmon. You need to try the candied salmon, it's an explosion for your taste buds!

Indigenous food is one of the only cuisines that is very unique to Canada and the origins of the country. It has deep cultural roots and is helping Indigenous communities recover parts of their culture that has been lost. It is definitely something that you should not pass up!

16. VERY VANCOUVER

Vancouver's own unique food scene has developed and changed to include and showcase not only well loved Canadian favourites but to also display a wide range of dishes from other cultures and cuisines. Vancouver has all the benefits of a bustling metropolitan hub but still retains it's unique food scene that is a combination of far off flavours and local staples with a twist - always fresh ingredients that are linked to the agricultural center of interior British Columbia and the Pacific Ocean. No matter where you go you are bound to be met with some fresh and explosive flavours.

Lots of people choose to migrate to the big city, from all across Canada and the world, with hopes and dreams of starting a business or local restaurant. These local businesses are well supported by Vancouverites and visitors to the cities who like to enjoy the creative dishes they serve. As they start to live and settle down in Canada you can often find these businesses popping up that not only serve food made in the traditional way but food with a twist. Of course I'm referring to fusion food! And Vancouver has some of the most interesting combinations you'll find across Canada!

Japadog is a hotdog stand/food truck that is truly unique to Vancouver. Since its creation in 2005 by a couple who immigrated from Japan to Vancouver it has exploded in popularity and now has 6 locations and a food Truck in Vancouver and 2 locations in California. So you might be asking, what exactly is a Japadog? It is exactly what it sounds like - a Japanese hotdog. They take typically eastern ingredients and toppings such as nori (dried seaweed), teriyaki sauce, kimchi and even shrimp tempura and Yakisoba noodles with a western staple food - the american hotdog. Of course you can swap out your beef dog for a veggie dog, bratwurst or a pork sausage if beef is not your thing. Nothing compliments the traditionally quick lunch food than an order of shichimi and garlic fries or aonori fries. Japadog is a great grab and go lunch idea if you're on a walk through the city or on your way to English Bay or Stanley Park.

Another aspect of the Vancouvers food scene is restaurants that have their roots firmly in British Columbia. Oftentimes these restaurants are started by a few locals who want to do something different and support their local economy. Since fresh fish, meat and vegetables are so abundant in British Columbia, most of these local restaurants have local food and sustainability at the heart of them.

One great restaurant with origins in BC is Tacofino. I purposely didn't include this in the Tacos with lime section because although their tacos are delicious and authentic I thought they also have an amazing Vancouver Island origin story. Tacofino had its humble start as a taco truck that was routinely parked in the back of a surf shop parking lot in Tofino, British Columbia. They served the surfers, locals and tourists alike with delicious, bold flavoured tacos that used local ingredients that would support local BC farmers. Supporting the local economy is a core value of Tacofino. They source their tuna from Vancouver island and their chicken from Chilliwack (a city 2 hours away from Vancouver). Since opening their doors in 2009, they now have 11 Vancouver locations, 1 Victoria location and the original Tacofino truck in Tofino, still going strong. Each location's menu varies a little bit, one location might have some different taco options than the other, this gives customers the option to try something new each time!

17. WALK DOWN MAIN

Main street is an up and coming neighbourhood of Vancouver featuring plenty of local businesses, restaurants, parks and cafes. It's not hard to find a great restaurant when you're exploring the Main street neighbourhood, it boasts interesting hole in the wall places, an Afghan culinary escape, authentic Cantonese restaurants and more. Walking down main will introduce you to some of the best restaurants in Vancouver.

On a quiet stretch of main street, if you look hard enough you'll stumble across Long's Noodle House. This hole in the wall restaurant dishes out fabulous Shanghainese food. They're famous for their soup dumplings (xiao long bao) and wine chicken, but I would go with the soup dumplings! A delicious hole in the wall with limited seating, will come with lines during peak hours, so the best time to visit is the off hours.

You're in for a treat when you visit East is East! Integrating local organic food with a host of eastern flavours while capturing the vibrant energy of the dhabbas (small street vendors that served travellers along the silk road) is their specialty. I highly recommend the chai feast tasting menu to get the full experience.

Sun Sui Wah is the place to experience authentic Cantonese fare prepared in a classic way. When they opened in 1988 they were one of the first Cantonese restaurants in Vancouver, and they've lasted through the years for a reason! You have to try the classic egg tarts, sui mai or their classic lunch bentos, it's like visiting Hong Kong without ever having to fly!

18. GASTOWN GREATS

Gastown is an incredibly historic neighbourhood in downtown. It started out as the original downtown core in 1867 and was nicknamed "gassy" (later Gastown) after a man named Jack Deighton, who came and opened the first saloon. Since it's days as a one horse town, it has grown and been preserved as a historic hub for restaurants, nightlife and businesses. Over the years there have been some wonderful restaurants that have come and established themselves in Gastown.

The water st cafe is one of the best places to eat in Gastown and has been around since 1988. With amazing views of the popular Gastown steam clock and elegant and cozy decor it's the perfect place to soak in the Gastown atmosphere! Try and grab a table by the window and see if you can catch the steam clock ringing and the tourists gathering every fifteen minutes or so. Did I mention they also host local live bands and artists on the second floor? So you can enjoy dinner and a show!

19. GROCERIES GALORE

Buying some groceries while visiting Vancouver might not be high on your priority list but sometimes it's a good way to save some money on your travels and it can be great in a pinch if you have to pick up a few things. Vancouver is well known for higher grocery prices so it can be good to know where to get the best price on certain items. Buy-Low Foods is the perfect stop if you're looking for affordable groceries and produce, they also have an extensive international section in case you want to try something new. IGA is a good mid range store with a good selection of groceries and deli, and somehow their produce is always ripe and ready to eat!

For a grocery store that's top tier you need to go to Choices, it's the Canadian version of Wholefoods. It's the best store to find organic and local produce and groceries and the food from their deli counter could rival any Vancouver restaurant. You won't find many regular brands of groceries here but smaller, local independent brands, but don't worry you can still find some familiar brands too.

20. FOOD TRUCK CITY

Vancouver means business when it comes to food trucks. You can find any kind of cuisine you would want with all the convenience of a food truck. Vancouver has some interesting food trucks to say the least! Have you ever wanted to try a breakfast food truck? Crack On is the perfect place if you love egg based breakfast sandwiches on toasted sourdough bread! The "crack sandwich" is great for those early morning walks!

Disco Cheetah is another food truck that can really hold a crowd. Their delicious and simple Korean bowls and salads make for a quick and easy lunch on the go without sacrificing any flavour. The Korean fried chicken bowl with chilli mayo will keep you coming back day after day. Last but not least the Holi Masala food truck does colourful and flavourful Indian food just like the name would suggest! In India Holi is the festival of colours and you can see people celebrating by throwing coloured powder in the air. Don't worry, you won't get hit with any colours here but the food will blow you away. Their curry bowls and kabob dogs are worth finding this food truck but what you really have to try is the mango lassi (sweet yogurt based drink).

21. FOOD TOURS

A food tour is the perfect way to sample many amazing restaurants and cafes all in one go! More often than not you will learn all the secret local spots, the history of the establishments and what makes the dishes so popular! If you are traveling on a budget or are short on time a food tour is a good option! Vancouver has lots of tour companies but the one you really want to pick is Secret Food Tours. They take you through the historic neighborhood of Gastown to sample Asian and Canadian cuisine as well as a heavily guarded "secret dish". You can upgrade your package if you want to try some delicious craft beers or ciders as well. You're guaranteed to come out with a wealth of knowledge about things you might not have gained roaming around on your own!

22. FESTIVALS AND EVENTS

Being such a multicultural city Vancouver is for sure going to have some binge worthy food festivals going on all year round! Planted expo sheds new light on all things plant based so if you're looking to try plant based food for the first time or you're looking to branch out this would be the festival for you. In the summer time The Greater Vancouver Food Truck Festival is also a great way to sample small plates from Vancouver's popular trucks all in one place!

In Richmond (part of the greater Vancouver area) you can find the Steveston Salmon Festival where they are here to celebrate all things salmon! You couldn't get any more Pacific NorthWest than this! Not only do they have amazing salmon based dishes but plenty of things to do and entertainment! It's worth the trip to Richmond.

23. THE MORE MARKETS THE MERRIER

Being a large city that's so close to natural resources and fresh produce of course Vancouver would be a hot spot for markets of all shapes and sizes! People love to get out on a Saturday or Sunday and explore the markets! People love visiting the Granville island market, one of the biggest and steadiest in the city. It's open Monday to Sunday and it's full of the best produce, fresh fish and delicious treats in the city! I'd recommend spending a few hours here sampling all the desserts (especially the Nanaimo bars). If you're feeling adventurous you can make your own charcuterie board with artisan cheese, meat (cured and smoked) and fresh fruit to enjoy with a view of Downtown Vancouver. You can find a seasonal rotating farmers market in various locations across the city like Riley park, west end, Hastings park etc that bring interesting food items and fresh veggies from all over the Fraser Valley area. Whichever market you pick it's going to make for a great afternoon!

24. SUPPORTING THE LOCALS

In Vancouver it's very easy to find big box stores and chain restaurants, anything you can find in Canada (and sometimes the USA) we have it too. It can be nice to visit a chain restaurant because you know what you're going to get and it's very consistent but what it lacks is authenticity and flavour. The best way to support local business is to eat, drink and shop locally. By avoiding the chain restaurants and box stores you are creating unique and interesting memories, and supporting the small businesses. In any neighbourhood in Vancouver it's very easy to spot the local shops selling wares or restaurants with home cooked food. Many of the tips I have included are local restaurants so you can feel good about where you visit. So please, stop in and enjoy Vancouver from a locals perspective.

25. CLASSY COCKTAILS

Time to grab some cocktails in style! Vancouver is well known as a filming hotspot and In this tip we visit some of the best bars to grab an evening cocktail. You're sure to feel like a true celebrity.

Uva Wine and Cocktail Bar is an award winning cocktail bar that offers a seasonal cocktail menu and a large wine selection. They are always serving something fresh and exciting. Their cocktail menu features some interesting ingredients like Greek yogurt, plum wine, and rose reduction. Each cocktail is carefully prepared by their skilled bartenders, it's amazing to watch them create your drink. They also have some small bites like smoked and cured meats and cheeses to share that pair nicely with your wine or cocktail. The cozy yet upscale decor will have you feeling like a Vancouver elite and the fantastic service will surely be the highlight of your night.

26. HAPPY HOUR

Happy hour is no joke here in Vancouver, there are lots of restaurants that offer happy hour deals on food and drink but these are the tried and true places with the best happy hour deals. Cannibal Cafe is a rock themed burger bar with vintage and eclectic decor, like their wall covered from top to bottom in artsy vintage looking posters. Their happy hour is from 4-6 and you can get a classic burger and fries for less than round trip bus fare. Drinks like sleeves of beer or whiskey shots are also on special. If you're feeling like some diner fare, the late afternoon is the best time to visit.

Colony Bar on Granville is a large bar with a modern industrial feel. If you feel like playing pool or skee ball or arcade games grab a few friends and a picnic table at Colony Bar and you're on your way. Their happy hour has a wider variety than Cannibal, with serious deals on sliders, nachos, tacos and more! You can add 1 oz well drinks (basic liquors), various beer and wine to the table as well without breaking the bank!

You can't get any better than tacos from the Pawn Shop YVR. This dimly lit dive bar will have you begging for a 5th chicken tinga taco and at their happy hour price you can't go wrong. They have some gluten free and vegetarian options as well so happy hour can be a real crowd pleaser. Their famous spiked slush is also on the happy hour menu so pick your liquor of choice and mix to create a custom drink of your own! My secret tip? Try to get a seat on their patio, the lively Granville atmosphere will really add to the experience.

27. A BREW OR TWO

Vancouver is the birthplace of the Canadian craft beer industry so naturally we would have some of the best craft breweries around. Sampling flights of craft beer is a favourite pastime for Vancouver locals, and it's the perfect way to pass an afternoon - rain or shine!

Main street brewing is your classic craft brewery that has an extensive tap list of delicious craft beers with mostly IPA's and sours, but there's a few ales and pilsners in there as well. Their industrial setting makes it a great spot to hangout and sample a flight of beer, if you don't mind the chatter.

33 Acres is another brewery that brews craft beer to perfection but their space reminds me more of a light, airy cafe. Their minimalist and stark white decor allows you to relax and enjoy what you're really there for - the beer. Their menu does not focus too heavily on one kind of beer but has a broad range of different styles and some ciders too, which makes it a great crowd pleaser.

Strange Fellows brewing is great if you're looking for a brewery that's more "out of the box". They focus on the strange and creative brews. They have a wide variety of craft beers as well as wine and cider. My favourite is the Madame Roxanne black raspberry sour, it makes a great sipping beer. They have a more modern industrial decor and a food menu that compliments their beers nicely.

28. VINEYARD VARIETIES

Although the Okanagan Region is world renowned for their wines and vineyards, most people don't know that there are wineries that are just as good and way closer to Vancouver. If you have a spare 12 hours to drive to the Oakanagan and back it's worth the visit, but just in case you are tight on time there are beautiful vineyards to visit that are closer to Vancouver. The nearby cities of Langley and Abbotsford are home to some of the best wineries in the province and they are only an hour drive from Vancouver.

The best vineyard in this area is the Glass House Estate Winery, right on the Canada/US border. The vineyard was started by a small family from the Netherlands in 1983 and has been growing ever since. They have delicious white wines as well as some sparkling, rose and red options that pair nicely with their brunch and dinner menu. Check out the greenhouse while you're here and enjoy a flight to sample their wines on their stone patio.

29. FARM TO TABLE

Who doesn't love a trip to the farm! You can pick up some local produce, dairy or meat and sometimes if you get lucky they're might be a shop with some home made goodies. Bonus if there's some cute animals to see or a petting area!

The area surrounding Vancouver is known for its vast farm lands so the fame options are endless. Although you could easily visit multiple farms there is a one stop shop farm that has it all, which is convenient if you're short on time.

Rondriso farm is about an hour outside Vancouver in Surrey and it makes a great day trip farm to try! Their pumpkin patch and bay rides in the fall really draw in a crowd and their general store is always packed full of local produce, meat and dairy products for you to take with you!

30. DAY TRIP EATS

Even though Vancouver is packed full of restaurant options, sometimes it can be nice to take a day trip and try something new! Vancouver is surrounded by many other cities that specialize in different types of cuisine. For example Surrey is a popular place for Indian food, Richmond can fill all your East Asian cravings and Port Moody is the place to find stellar craft beers. All of these cities are within an hour drive from downtown Vancouver and any one of them (or all) can make your trip worthwhile!

In Surrey you need to try Apna Chaat House, trust me you're in for a treat. Don't let the basic exterior fool you, this place is well known for its delicious Indian Chaat. What is Chaat? It is a simple but filling snack that is served out of push carts in many cities in India. You can find butter chicken or biryani at any Indian restaurant but it takes a good eye to find a place that does street food just right!

In Richmond the place to be is Shanghai River! They are locally famous for their daily dim sum and dumplings, which are authentic to the South of China. Dim sum is the best way to try authentic Chinese food, because it allows you to try many little dishes at once. You have to try the pan fried noodles or pork dumplings (and bring some home for later!).

Port Moody is a beautiful little town and you would often forget just how close it is to Vancouver, you can even reach it by public transit! Along Murray st there are 6 breweries all in a row, which make it easy to bar hop through the area! I like to start at Moody ales and buy flights at each brewery so that way, you can sample more than just one or two! If you catch a beautiful sunny day in Vancouver, patio hopping in Port Moody is what you need to be doing!

31. A FINE TASTE IN COFFEE

Canada comes in at number 10 on the list of the world's biggest coffee consumers and it is the only non-European country to make the top 10! Canucks really do enjoy their daily double-double (a 20oz coffee with two shots of sugar and cream) from Tim Hortons but in Vancouver, coffee culture takes on a whole new meaning. In Vancouver artisan coffee shops serving up organic, fair trade and locally roasted coffee are in abundance. Scattered all over the city you are sure to find a local coffee shop and whether you're looking for a quiet place to read, study or meet friends, there are cafes for everyone! Although trying a double-double is an essential experience (especially if this is your first time visiting Canada), I suggest you try one of these local cafes instead!

Timbertrain is a local Vancouver cafe that flaunts high ceilings, wood floors and massive windows in its Gastown location. Operating out of a heritage building (which Vancouver is known for) gives this cafe a historic feeling. Their train carriage compartment style seating will have you feeling like you are stepping back in time. They are known best for their pour over style coffee which is made from ethically sourced beans. Timbertrain pays great attention to the sustainability practices that are taking place all the way from the farm to your cup!

Prado cafe is a local staple that started as a single store on commercial drive and has grown to have 7 locations. Their light and airy vibe give you a sense of calm as you walk in. It's the perfect place for a quiet date, study session or a meet up with friends. Grab a latte and a butter croissant and relax!

Their There is what you get when you mix elegance, a coffee focused cafe and comfort food!

The cafe with a confusing name is a laid back, bright and trendy atmosphere where you can enjoy expertly brewed coffee, classy wines or a crispy chicken burger. Yes I said chicken burger! It's a great blend of delicious comfort food, trendy decor and a relaxing atmosphere.

Last but not least we have Pallet Coffee Roasters. Pallet brings specialty coffee to your local neighbourhood with it's friendly baristas, delicious coffee and laid back atmosphere. It has a bright and airy space with a slight industrial feel, which makes it a perfect place to bring friends and hangout for a while. Pallet has been around since 2014 which makes it an established cafe (so you know it's good).

32. DID YOU SAY BRUNCH?

Can't lie, who doesn't love a good kinda healthy kinda greasy brunch? Whether you're recovering from the night before or starting off tonight on the right foot you're going to want to find the perfect brunch restaurant because lots of restaurants in the city offer brunch which can make deciding on a place difficult.

It doesn't have to be difficult, any of these restaurants make a delicious spot for a bunch.

Jam Cafe always has a long line outside for brunch on the weekends but I promise you it is worth the wait! Heavily inspired but Southern cuisine their menu features fried chicken, cornbread and buttermilk biscuits so you know it's gotta be great comfort food. The dining area is always alive with happy guests! It makes a great place for a good pick me up brunch.

The Red Wagon is your classic no-nonsense breakfast and lunch diner. They have classic breakfast items but lots of interesting items for vegetarians like the tofu scramble or a falafel sandwich! It's great if you are visiting and you have dietary restrictions, and it's great even if you don't! Did you know they cure and smoke their own meats in-house? You really need to try something on the menu that features their smoked or cured meat. My go to would be the croque monsieur.

I saved one of the most interesting brunch restaurants for last. At ARC restaurant on the weekends you can get bottomless brunch for a set price. Yes you heard that correctly - bottomless. Sample all their delicious breakfast favourites: salmon benedict: liege waffles and their ooey gooey skillet (my favourite). It's a brunch lover's dream come true!

33. BREAK FOR LUNCH

After breakfast you're going to need lunch right? Lunch is typically short and sweet, something you could eat on the go if you really needed too. These takeout spots make the perfect lunch on the go, so you can get back to exploring and enjoying the sights of Vancouver!

Meat and Bread is the perfect no nonsense sandwich shop in Downtown Vancouver with multiple locations. If you're craving something fast and quick they have great options like a porchetta sandwich, buffalo chicken or a classic grilled cheese, and you can pair those with some sides or a dessert. They do have some quick dine in seats but their sandwiches pair best with a view of the Vancouver harbour (which is only steps away from their Pender location).

You can find another quick lunch pick me up at one of the many Tractor locations. They specialize in protein-packed healthy sandwiches, bowls or wraps. They have many vegan/vegetarian options as well as wholesome meat options. In most tractor locations you can choose to dine in or take your meal to go.

34. IT'S FINE TO DINE

Fine dining in style is surely a treat and what better time to do it than when you're travelling? A night out at a fancy restaurant is the perfect experience to have to top off a wonderful trip and there's no better place to do it than Brix and Mortar. This restaurant is tucked away in downtown Vancouver away from the crowds inside a heritage building from 1912. The low lit and elegant atmosphere is the right environment to sample one (or two) of their 60 wines and taste the local halibut or blackened duck. Here you are sure to have an exceptional fine dining experience.

35. SWEET TREATS

A sweet treat seems to always hit the spot! Vancouver is full of delectable desserts and millions of options to choose from. Although Vancouver has many many options to choose from there are a few places in the city that are a must visit! Popina Canteen's puff creams are a dream come true on Granville Island. This small little canteen not only has beautiful views of downtown Vancouver but they also have the most delicious soft serve ice cream served in a cream puff! Delicious combinations like Bees Knees and Turkish delight are sure to intrigue and delight your taste buds. Another cool spot in the city is Made by Mister in Yaletown. Here they create interesting and artisanal ice cream flavours that are then frozen using liquid nitrogen that allows for a denser richer texture. They even make in house ice cream sandwiches that are out of this world.

If you in the mood for something sweeter but lighter you have to try a bubble tea from Sun Tea. They have many options to choose from, milk tea, fruit tea, fruit slushies and more! You can even grab a cute baby pancake on the side! They have a few to go locations across the city, and it makes a nice addition to a neighbourhood walk!

36. DONUT MISS OUT

Donuts are a delicious, sweet pick me up and if you get the right one they can be an outstanding treat. Of course every cafe might have a version of a donut for you to sample, but the best donuts can be found at Lucky's donuts. Lucky's is a sub brand of Parallel 49, a famous local cafe in Vancouver. You can find their delicious donuts in the pastry case, and they have many options to choose from. If you like traditional donuts you can grab an old fashioned or a french cruller and if you're looking for something more adventurous you should try the Vegan Gluten free triple chocolate or the dirty chai bismarck. Their donuts are made fresh throughout the day so no worries about getting a stale one! Their attentive team is baking constantly. They also pair well with a coffee or tea from Parallel 49!

37. LEAVE ROOM FOR DESSERT

Some would argue that dessert is the best part of the meal, and I would have to agree. Sometimes you just need that delicious kick of sugar after a meal! Why should you go to a restaurant specifically for dessert when most restaurants offer a dessert menu? Well, you know if it's a dessert only restaurant that they must be doing something right if they remain open with a limited food menu.

True Confections is the place to stop after dinner to cure your cake craving! They have so many cakes and pies to choose from that you might be there for a while. The New York style cheesecake is exceptional and it's the "pièce de résistance" (the chief dish of a meal).

38. KIDS TABLE

Dining out with children while away on a trip is almost unavoidable. While there are plenty of restaurant options it's hard to know which ones are child friendly. Is the music too loud? No high chairs?

Plenty of breakables or places to get lost? So many things to consider.

Pizzaria Barbarella is not only a fun name to sound out but has all your child related needs covered. They have plenty of highchairs as well as plastic utensils and sippy cups, plus what kid doesn't love pizza?

Bells and Whistles is another great option for kids young and old. Plenty of stroller parking for the young ones and skee ball arcade games for the older ones (and mom and dad). The picnic style tables are perfect for families and the colourable origami game sheets are a perfect take home. The kids will be begging you to come back again!

39. A GREASY SPOON

We all love a good greasy meal every now and then, it feeds the soul and something about it just feels good. It can't just be any old greasy spoon, it has to taste good too. Down low chicken shack does crispy and tasty chicken that's fried to perfection! Who needs 11 herbs and spices when you have lemon pepper, jerk or cool ranch (just to name a few). Their never frozen chicken sandwiches will have you coming back again and again.

If you're feeling something less chicken heavy, Score on Davie is the perfect cozy pub and their fare is done just right. The lively pub atmosphere, daily drink specials and pulled pork Mac and cheese is the perfect combo for an awesome night out.

40. THE PERFECT PIZZA

The perfect pizza can be hard to nail down. Everyone seems to like it differently, thin crust, Italian style, vegan cheese and some even go so far as to use ranch instead of marinara sauce. Vancouver has a pizza scene that rivals NYC, but instead of 99 cent pizza on every corner they have a wealth of pizza centered restaurants that have options to please everyone's tastes. Virtuous pie is a vegan pizza joint that has all the comforts and flavours you would expect in a regular pizza place! They have many gluten free spicy and nut free pies that will please even the biggest of meat eaters.

Nook is the place to go if you are looking for hearty, traditional Italian pizzas that stick to your ribs and have you craving more. Their ingredients are so fresh they practically jump off the pizza, and their tasty add ons make every dish customizable.

I took a stab at NYC in the beginning so it's only fair I mention the most authentic New York Style pizza that you can find in Vancouver. You need to go to Aj's Brooklyn Pizza Joint to get an authentic NYC slice! Created by a Brooklyn local, who claims to have eaten a slice of Brooklyn pizza every day before dinner, it's safe to say they know pizza. Come and have a slice and feel like you're a part of a local Brooklyn community!

41. VERY VEGAN

Vegan food is on the rise across the world and it has definitely gained traction in Vancouver. Lots of people who live in Vancouver are vegan (or vegetarian) and even those who are not are likely to try, and enjoy, a vegan meal on occasion. With the rise of popular trends such as "Veganuary" and

"Meatless Mondays" vegan food is on the rise. Vegan-related searches in Vancouver surged by 28% year-over-year in 2020.

You can easily find vegan versions of classic favourites in every restaurant but the best way to try some delicious and unique vegan food would be to head to a specialty vegan restaurant. The Acorn, named the best vegan eatery in the world, is a fine dining vegan experience boasting creative dishes from locally sourced ingredients. It is bound to please even the heaviest of meat eaters.

For a hearty vegan mid range option would be the Vegan Cave Cafe has some classic favourites like pizza and burritos but healthier options such as salads and bowls it's a popular choice in the Gastown neighbourhood.

Kokomo is classic vegan food with a menu loaded with vegan smoothie options and healthy, nutrient packed bowls and salads. If you are looking for a healthy, lighter option Kokomo is the place to go.

42. DINE ON DOSAS

Dosas are a dish that is unique to the South of India. Dosa became popular in Vancouver after It is a thin pancake made from a fermented batter. The fillings are called masala dosas and they are usually filled with flavourful vegetables and spices like cumin and turmeric. You can find many variations of the dosa filling and many restaurants will have 7 or more options. The dosa exploded in popularity after a Kerala immigrant, Raj Muttavanchery, opened House of Dosas. He had a special price on Monday's which drew in the customers and that was the end of that. You can find this dosa restaurant on the Kingsway and be sure to stop in and try the ghee roast dosa or a paneer (indian cheese) masala dosa for a real taste of South India.

43. REAL RAMEN:

With Vancouver being a very rainy and cooler coastal city it's no wonder this hot Japanese noodle soup is a staple here. From traditional pork ramen to unique twists like vegan ramen, you can find ramen spots on every corner of the city. Vancouver even has a "Ramen row" in the West end along Robson st in-between Denman st and Thurlow st. It's quite easy to stumble into a Ramen restaurant on a cool and overcast day but it's worth the hunt to get to the best ones.

Kintaro ramen is the city's oldest ramen restaurant and it's lasted through the years for a good reason! They have plenty of options like vegetarian ramen and spicy ramen!

Danbo Ramen is another Vancouver classic. This restaurant's specialty is Fukuoka Tonkotsu Ramen which originated in Kurume in the Fukuoka region of Japan in 1947, and was created completely by accident. This accident exploded in popularity and has since spread all over the world. It is a no frills ramen with thinner noodles, and a secret milky pork bone broth. Danbo is definitely the best place to grab a warm bowl of tradition.

Hokkaido Ramen Santouka on Vancouver's "Ramen Row" is the perfect place for traditional Northern Japanese style ramen. It opened in 1980 with one mission, to serve delicious ramen. They have been serving up warm bowls ever since (with a pickled plum at the bottom). These restaurants are bound to warm your insides and make your taste buds sing!

44. TACOS WITH LIME

Vancouver is known for being a host to food from all around the world but what people don't know is that it's taco scene is booming. Tacos are a very popular meal or late night snack for Vancouverites. Nothing seems to hit the spot like a comforting and authentic Mexican taco. What goes into an authentic taco you might ask? You need to look for corn tortillas! Small corn tortillas are used in traditional Mexican tacos and they seem to hold up better than their wheat cousins. They also add to the freshness and flavour of the overall taco. Another thing to look for would be properly spiced meat and fresh cool veggies. The meat has to be marinated and cooked well (but not too well) and retain the juice and flavour. If your taco isn't dripping it's not authentic! Don't forget the lime wedge!

Here are the perfect places in Vancouver to find an authentic (and dripping) taco!

Chancho tortilleria create a small Mexican town kind of authenticity through their native or ancient corn that is ground to make their tortillas. They are passionate about corn! They import non gmo corn from over 32 indigenous communities near Oaxaca. Not to mention these varieties aren't found anywhere else in the world. You can truly say it's a one of a kind experience to try their tacos! I would recommend their Panza tacos or some take home tortillas for you to create your own!

45. SUSTAINABLE MEALS

Steps away from the beautiful Kitsilano beach you can find some authentic Mexican tacos that are made with sustainable seafood, meat and produce. They have deals every day of the week but you have to go for Taco Tuesday if you can. Try the baja pescado or spicy chorizo for something hearty and comforting or the grilled corn or crispy cauliflower for something a little lighter (only a little).

46. CHARCUTERIE ISN'T ONLY FOR THE FRENCH

Charcuterie is a beautiful part of french cuisine which is typically a board made up of cured meats and fine cheeses, with some bread or olives. Modern charcuterie boards include nuts, fruits, veggies, vegan meats and anything your heart desires. It is the perfect meal to share with friends over a nice glass of wine and can be the start of a fun evening. Au Comptoir is an upscale French restaurant in the Kitsilano neighbourhood of Vancouver. The modern yet comforting deecor will make you feel like you're eating in a small cafe in Paris. Not only do they have drool worthy French menu items like croque monsieur and duck confit but it is the place to visit for a traditional French charcuterie board. You can experience a little slice of France by pairing it with a glass of pinot noir.

47. INEXPENSIVE FAVORITES

Jules Bistro is an inexpensive option that still gets you some fine charcuterie in a French Bistro atmosphere. Go for happy hour (2:30 pm - 5:30 pm) to sample some of their delicious feature wines with a regular charcuterie board, cheese board or truffle fries. Chef andOwner Emmanuel Joinville opened Jules Bistro in 2007 and has been serving the locals fine french cuisine with a west coast twist ever since. He likes to source all of his ingredients from local vendors in and around the Vancouver area.

48. MEAT LOVERS PARADISE

Who doesn't love a good meat dish? Canadians are well known for having meat as a staple at almost every meal and even though times are changing and vegetarian options are gaining popularity, restaurants that can cook the perfect steak are persevering! One in particular that comes to mind is Gotham steakhouse in downtown Vancouver. Not only can they cook a grade A steak perfection but they also have delicious smoked salmon, milk fed veal, caviar

and oysters that make a delicious main when paired
with a side like the field mushrooms or baked Idaho
potato. The servers are plenty and are more than
happy to assist with anything too may need, It's an
upscale dining experience like none other.

49. CHINATOWN FAVOURITES

Chinatown is a popular area in Vancouver for
locals and visitors alike, the atmosphere is alive with
people out grocery shopping or visiting local shops
and restaurants. First established in the 1890's
Chinatown has been buzzing with bright colours,
smells and sounds. Vancouver experienced a wave of
Chinese immigration as the Trans-Canada railway
was created, offering many jobs. Chinatown is filled
with classic asian stores, architecture, art and culture.
It's the 3rd best Chinatown in North America, right
after New York and San Francisco. Dim Sum is a
popular dish to get in Chinatown, typically consisting
of many different small plates of food to be shared
with the table. Jade Dynasty does dimsum perfectly,
serving dim sum throughout the day. Shrimp

dumplings, spring rolls, steamed buns and egg tarts for dessert sounds delicious (don't worry I wont say anything if you choose to eat dessert first).

While you are spending some time in Chinatown go visit New Town Bakery and Cafe on Pender st. Their Hong Kong milk tea and flavourful steamed buns make a nice light lunch and a good excuse to take a break!

At night time Keefer bar is alive and kicking. This is a popular apothecary style bar offers cocktails infused with asian flavours and their small sharing plates are complementary to the drinks. The friendly bartenders can help you find the perfect cocktail that suits your tastes and Keefer Yard will keep you entertained all night with their mini golf course, right in the middle of the bar! It's the perfect way to spend a night out in Chinatown.

50. EATING FROM AROUND THE WORLD

The Vancouver food scene is outstanding when it comes to diversity. You can go just about anywhere in the city and find a restaurant that makes you feel like you've travelled to the other side of the world, and I'm not just talking about the usual Italian, Indian, Chinese or French cuisines here. Vancouver has some truly unique cuisines from countries around the world just waiting to be discovered (and shared).

The first restaurant I want to highlight is Transylvanian traditions bakery in Davie Village. They offer an amazing variety of pastries, cakes and other goodies from Transylvania and other Eastern European countries. Have you ever tried a Dobos cake? It's a layered cake with Nutella, chocolate creams and butter cream! You're bound to love it! Kürtőskalács is a popular pastry otherwise known as chimney cakes. You can eat and unravel them after they are rolled in sugar! It makes a great dessert.

Afghan horseman is a popular Afgani restaurant on south Granville st. Here you can experience a world of flavours from Afghanistan in a traditional setting. The decor really sets the mood for a juicy kebab platter with all the fixings. Make sure to order a humous or sabzi mast for the table, it makes a great addition! Afghan horseman has been open since 1974 and it was Canada's first Afghan restaurant!

Have you ever heard of Australian cuisine? Take a trip down under to Moose's Down Under! This restaurant makes you feel like you're in an Australian bar, and it's the perfect place to try an Australian meat pie with an Aussie beer on the side. If you're feeling super adventurous try their "Roo burger" it's exactly what you think it is - kangaroo meat! It's like a little piece of Australia right here in Vancouver.

BONUS UNIQUE SPACES

Dining can be taken to a whole other level when the space that you are eating with is an experience in itself. These restaurants pair an amazing dining experience when it comes to the food and service but with the addition of a unique space to dine in! Grab your camera and come along for some cool selfies at these Vancouver restaurants!

Start off (or end) your evening with a cocktail at Key party. It is a cozy and intimate speakeasy hidden behind the front of an accountants office in Mt Pleasant. The dim lights, tasty cocktails and dark decor make it the best place for a pair or small group. Don't forget to check out the intriguing mural behind the bar.

The Eatery is a truly wild sushi experience. Not only is the sushi top notch but it's served in what looks like a neon underwater theme park. Be sure to go after dark to see it in its full effect with the black light! Snap a picture through their gallery window or with some eclectic ceiling decorations for a memento of the evening.

These two restaurants are sure to make one heck of an adventurous evening and I'm sure you won't have a more unique dining experience anywhere else!

TOP 3 REASONS TO VISIT VANCOUVER

1) **Cultural Diversity**: Vancouver is filled to the brim with local and forigen culture that's just waiting to be explored. It doesn't matter what kind of cuisine you love or if you like fine dining or dive bars, Vancouver caters to it all! As you've seen throughout this book, this is just the tip of the iceberg in terms of what Vancouver's culinary scene has to offer.

2) **Proximity to nature:** With the mountains to the north and west, Pacific ocean to the east, there is no shortage of natural places to explore in Vancouver. More often than not you don't even have to leave the city limits to escape from it all. With hundreds of hiking trails and outdoor activities to do here, you could never get bored.

3) **History:** Founded in 1886, Vancouver quickly grew from a busy community of the Coast Salish people and some small logging ports to a huge city after the completion of the Trans Canada Railway and the steamships that linked Asia and the rest of the world to Canada. There is an abundance of history whether it be natural, cultural or modern to uncover here in Vancouver.

READ OTHER BOOKS BY CZYK PUBLISHING

Eat Like a Local United States Cities & Towns

Eat Like a Local United States

Eat Like a Local- Oklahoma: Oklahoma Food Guide

Eat Like a Local- North Carolina: North Carolina Food Guide

Eat Like a Local- New York City: New York City Food Guide

Children's Book: Charlie the Cavalier Travels the World by Lisa Rusczyk

Eat Like a Local

Follow *Eat Like a Local on* Amazon.
Join our mailing list for new books

http://bit.ly/EatLikeaLocalbooks

CZYKPublishing.com

Printed in Great Britain
by Amazon

37918984R00056